Signs

in the

Heavens

*An End Time Scenario Played Out in the Clouds
Over Rochester, New York, June 22, 2018*

SIGNS IN THE HEAVENS - An End Time Scenario
Played Out in the Clouds over Rochester, NY, June 22, 2018
Copyright © 2019 by Allan Miller

Printed in the USA
ISBN 978-1-941173-39-8
1. Eschatology   2. Inspirational

Published by

Olive **P**ress Messianic and Christian Publisher
www.olivepresspublisher.com
olivepressbooks@gmail.com

Messianic & Christian Publisher

Our prayer at Olive Press is that we may help make the Word of Adonai fully known, that it spread rapidly and be glorified everywhere. We hope our books help open people's eyes so they will turn from darkness to Light and from the power of the adversary to God and to trust in יֵשׁוּעַ Yeshua (Jesus). (From II Thess. 3:1; Col. 1:25; Acts 26:18,15 NRSV *New Revised Standard Version* and CJB) May this book in particular reveal more deep meaning in the Jewish roots of our faith.

Contents

Introduction

This is about a series of cloud formation photos taken on the morning of June 22, 2018, in the skies over Rochester, New York. They paint a picture of an End Time Scenario found in the Bible, the Word of GOD. I will share the scenario here using the photographs and what I see as related Scriptures from GOD's Word.

Are you ready?

Scene 1
The Cross

Ephesians 2:13-16 *But now, you who were once far off have been brought near through the shedding of the MESSIAH's blood. 14) For He Himself is our Shalom — He has made us both one and has broken down the M'chitzah, (Divider) which divided us 15) by destroying in His own body the enmity occasioned by the Torah (Law), with its commands set forth in the form of ordinances. He did this in order to create in union with Himself from the two groups (Jew and Gentile) a single new humanity and thus make Shalom, 16) and in order to reconcile to GOD both in a single body by being*

executed on a stake (Cross) as a criminal and thus Himself killing that enmity.

MESSIAH crucified:
1-) Our hope of Glory (Colossians 1:27)
2-) The beginning of the End Times

Who is the MESSIAH?
Colossians 1:14-20 *It is through His (GOD's) Son that we have redemption — that is, our sins have been forgiven. 15) He (YESHUA/JESUS) is the visible image of the invisible GOD. He is supreme over all creation, 16) because in connection with Him were created all things — in Heaven and on earth.... (skip to) 18) Also He is Head of the body, the Messianic Community (Church) — He is the beginning, the firstborn from the dead, so that He might hold first place in everything. 19) For it pleased GOD to have HIS full Being live in HIS Son 20) and through HIS Son to reconcile to Himself all things, whether on earth or in Heaven, making peace through Him, through having HIS Son shed His blood by being executed on a stake (Cross).*

YESHUA/JESUS is GOD's Son, born to die for humanity's sins on the execution stake, the cross. When I saw the cross in the sky, YESHUA/JESUS came to mind.

His death and resurrection began the End Times.

The next photo is a GOD edit of the cross photograph. Why a GOD edit? God commands the winds, and the wind moved the form of the cross just enough to create the next picture.

Scene 2

An Angel:

God's Word, the Bible, has a lot to say about angels in the End Times. Angels are GOD's messengers, angels minister to believers in YESHUA/JESUS. Angels are written about a lot in the Book of the Revelation, the last book in the Bible, the book of the End Times.

The Revelation 14:6-7 *Next I saw another angel flying in mid-heaven with everlasting Good News to proclaim to those living on the earth — to every nation, tribe, language and people. 7) In a loud voice he said, "Fear GOD, give HIM Glory, For the hour has come when HE will pass judgment! Worship the One who made Heaven and earth, the sea and the springs of water!"*

Another angel will come on the scene and will have some dealings with the image of the next scene I saw in the sky.

Scene 3

The Dragon:

(A note of explanation first. The dragon I am about to write about from the Book of the Revelation in no way looks like the photograph. You will notice that as soon as you read the text. But the picture of the dragon I saw in the cloud will work for my purpose here.)

The Revelation 12:1-8 *Now a great sign was seen in Heaven — a woman clothed with the sun, under her feet the moon, and on her head a crown of twelve stars. 2) She was pregnant and about to give birth, and she screamed in the agony of labor. 3) Another sign was seen in Heaven: there was a great red dragon with seven heads and ten horns, and on its head were seven royal crowns. 4) Its tail swept a third of the stars out of Heaven and threw them down to the earth. ... (Skip to) 7) Next there was a battle in Heaven — Mikha-el (Michael) and his angels fought against the dragon, and the dragon and his angels fought back. 8) But it was not strong enough to win, so that there was no longer any place for them in Heaven.*

There is a lot more about the dragon but to find out about it you will have to read the rest of chapter twelve.

Now let's see what chapter 20, verses 1-3 have to add.

1) Next I saw an angel coming down from Heaven, who had the key to the Abyss and a great chain in his hand. 2) He seized the dragon, that ancient serpent, who is the devil and Satan [the adversary], and chained him up for a thousand years. 3) He threw him into the Abyss, locked it and sealed it over him; so that he could not deceive the nations any more until the thousand years were over. After that he has to be set free for a little while.

Let's move on to the next scene which can be seen in the next photo, and can be found in chapter 19 of the Revelation.

Scene 4

The Heavenly Choir:

The Revelation 19:6-9 *Then I heard what sounded like the roar of a huge crowd, like the sound of rushing waters, like loud peals of thunder, saying, "Hallelujah! ADONAI, GOD of Heaven's armies has begun HIS reign! 7) Let us rejoice and be glad! Let us give HIM Glory! For the time has come for the wedding of the Lamb, and His Bride has prepared herself— fine linen, bright and clean has been given her to wear." ("Fine linen" means the righteous deeds of GOD's people.) 9) The angel said to me, "Write: 'How blessed are those who have been invited to the wedding feast of the Lamb!'" Then he added, "These are GOD's very words."*

WHO IS THE LAMB'S BRIDE?

All of those who have put their faith/trust in YESHUA/ JESUS and His atoning work of salvation on the execution stake, the cross.

The last photograph depicts a scene that many believers in YESHUA/JESUS believe will happen before the scenes shared above: A "catching away" of all who have trusted in YESHUA/JESUS from day one until the day He comes for His bride. Our hope is found in the first letter of Paul to the believers in Thessalonica, - in chapter four of 1 Thessalonians, starting with verse 13, we read.

13) Now brothers, we want you to know the truth about those who have died; otherwise, you might become sad the way other people 14) do who have nothing to hope for. For since we believe that YESHUA/JESUS died and rose again, we also believe that in the same way GOD, through YESHUA/ JESUS, will take with Him those who have died. 15) When we say this, we base it on the Lord's own word: we who remain alive when the Lord comes will certainly not take precedence over those who have died. 16) For the Lord Himself will come down from Heaven with a rousing cry, with a call from one of the ruling angels, and with GOD's Shofar; those who died united with the MESSIAH will be the first to rise; 17) Then we who are left still alive will be caught up with them in the clouds to meet the Lord in the air; and thus we will always be with the Lord.

This End Time event is called:

Scene 5
The Rapture:

verse 18 closes out this portion of the scenario.

18) So encourage each other with these words.

Are you ready?

HOW DOES A PERSON COME TO YESHUA/JESUS?

The person who comes to YESHUA/JESUS to find forgiveness of their sins must first:

1- Believe...that He is who the Bible says He is, GOD's only begotten Son. (John 3:16)

2- By Faith/Trust...believe that He died to forgive us our sins, then was resurrected from death to give everlasting life to all who by Faith/Trust would...

3- Receive Him into their heart and life, and live for Him and with Him on a daily basis.

If you, the reader believe this and would like to invite YESHUA/JESUS to come into your heart and life, and live for Him, pray the short prayer that follows, from an honest heart.

Dear Lord YESHUA/JESUS, I believe that you are the Son of GOD. I believe that you came to earth to die for me and my sins. I believe that GOD raised you from the grave to live forever more. I ask you now to forgive me of all the sins that I have committed. I ask you to come into my heart and save me. I now commit my life to You. Help me to live for you now, that I may live with You forever. In Your Name I ask. Amen

THANK YOU YESHUA/JESUS

If you just asked YESHUA/JESUS to come into your heart and life, PRAISE GOD!!!

Welcome to the family of GOD. It doesn't end here though. To live every day for the Lord, a few things are necessary for you to do.

1. You will need to read the Bible daily to grow strong in your new faith.

2. You will need to obey the things you read in the Bible, GOD's Word.

3. You need to find a good Bible teaching Congregation... a community of believers to grow with.

4. You need to talk to GOD on a daily basis, prayer. He's always available to listen to you. He's waiting to hear from you.

5. You need fellowship with others who have trusted YESHUA/JESUS for salvation, brothers and sisters in the MESSIAH to pray with, and to study the Bible with during the week. It all helps you grow in your faith/trust in the Lord.

In closing:
The Grace of our Lord YESHUA the MESSIAH be with you all.

KEEP LOOKING UP!!!

www.ingramcontent.com/pod-product-compliance
Lightning Source LLC
Chambersburg PA
CBHW051242020426
42331CB00016B/3484